ASHLEY KIRKHAM

THE
VOICE
REVEALED

Transformation through singing

Mereo Books

Mereo Books 2nd Floor, 6-8 Dyer Street,
Cirencester, Gloucestershire, GL7 2PF

An imprint of Memoirs Book Ltd. www.mereobooks.com

THE VOICE REVEALED: 978-1-86151-948-1

Ashley Kirkham can be contacted by email vocaltutor@gmail.com
Or you can see more on Facebook @specialistvocaltutor

First published in Great Britain in 2019
by Mereo Books, an imprint of Memoirs Books Ltd.

Copyright ©2019

Ashley Kirkham has asserted his right under the Copyright Designs and Patents Act
1988 to be identified as the author of this work.

A CIP catalogue record for this book is available from the British Library.
This book is sold subject to the condition that it shall not by way of trade or
otherwise be lent, resold, hired out or otherwise circulated without the publisher's
prior consent in any form of binding or cover, other than that in which it is published
and without a similar condition, including this condition being imposed on the
subsequent purchaser.

The address for Memoirs Books Ltd. can be
found at www.memoirspublishing.com

Memoirs Books Ltd. Reg. No. 7834348

Typeset in 11/15pt Century Schoolbook
by Wiltshire Associates Ltd.
Printed and bound in Great Britain

For Clare and Robert

For Clara and Robert

Your voice is connected to everything you are, so discover who you are first, and then your voice will be revealed to you.

Ashley Kirkham

CONTENTS

Introduction
Acknowledgements

1. WHAT THIS BOOK IS ABOUT

2. BREATH

3. SOUND

4. WORDS

5. THE INVISIBLE CRAFT

6. PERFORMANCE

7. TEACHING

INTRODUCTION

Very early in my life, I started a journey. It was a journey to find myself, although I didn't know I was looking. I did know that I wanted to sing, so I searched and studied and practised until I met a singing teacher who showed me how to find me. From this place I watched the singing sing itself, unhindered and released from the clutches of the ego which thought it new better. Once I had found myself and the singing had come as a consequence of that, both became transformed. The process and consequences have been so transformational to me that I have since felt a very powerful desire to help others experience the same.

From an early age I had been fascinated by singers.

I seemed to have a natural facility for recognising what was good in singing and what was a poor imitation. My earliest recollections were of Danny Kaye, Mario Lanza, Paul Robeson, Oliver Hardy, Richard Lewis and my own dad, who was a very accomplished natural tenor who sang both popular and classical songs. My mum also sang to me when I was a young child, and although she wasn't the most technically proficient, she had a wonderful storytelling manner.

Because of this, I was already beginning to realise that singing took many forms, and I was also to discover over the years that followed that there was a great deal of confusion and ignorance regarding singing. Even singers who were immensely talented could often not help, because they often understood very little about what they did themselves when they sang.

Whilst studying at college, I found a lack of any consistent message from the collective vocal teachers. Every teacher had a different approach to the singing process, yet here they all were in the same place teaching from different hymn books. Of course, variety is the spice of life and it is very refreshing to have different personalities delivering a message with their own idiosyncrasies and emphasis, but this was not the case here.

At college there were many talented musicians with the sort of wealth and experience that was immeasurably invaluable to performers in that setting, many of whom I have the utmost respect for. The fact remained however, that the more I studied and listened and read and spoke to the very able singers and teachers, the more I came to realise that there was a pattern to what was happening under the surface, and I became more and more determined to unravel and define it.

The specific difficulty in teaching singing compared to all other instruments lies in the fact that the singer's instrument is inside them and is integrally connected to who they are and how they interact with their environment and themselves. The more I observed, the more I began to grasp the fact that virtually all the singers who made it because of their singing ability were essentially natural to varying degrees, and up to a point would sing well regardless of their teacher.

When I was about twenty years old, I was working with my good accompanist friend Gwen Jones. She mentioned she could arrange a meeting for me with a friend of hers called Dan Gregory. She told me that he was a great singer who had spent much of his career singing as a cathedral soloist and that he was very knowledgeable about singing and might be able to give me some advice. I jumped at the chance, and the first of many meetings was arranged.

Dan was ninety-one years old when I first met him. He had a magnificent bass voice with a two-and-a-half octave range, and he was to turn my life upside down regarding the entire craft of singing. My reason for singing also changed; it became a process of self-realisation and an appreciation of the craft and its transformational power. I continued to see Dan weekly over several years until his death at the age of ninety-eight. At times it was very difficult, and I felt very alone, but I knew deep within me that life had given me an incredible opportunity to interact with a very rare human being and the knowledge he had to share.

So, what was this knowledge? How was it gained? and why was this man not famous or rich, or even well known? Dan's knowledge was in fact gained through adversity. He had lost his family when he was only a young boy and was brought up by his aunt. Having a raw talent for singing and no money, he pursued the art through his own study and effort. He had his back to the wall in a time of severe poverty, but he had a desire to advance himself, along with the good fortune not to have been taught any accepted techniques that might have limited his outlook by any preconditioning.

He told me that he must have had within him the seeds of truth and was fortunate enough to have been placed in conditions that allowed those seeds to grow and flourish. Now that I have studied the concepts of quantum physics, spirituality and the natural laws of the universe, I see that Dan's teachings were no more than the universal laws conveyed by enlightened souls through time. What is unique is that he found a way to understand these laws as they related to singing.

A crucial factor that I feel made Dan so special was his utter lack of desire to earn money or fame for his abilities. Although I offered on many occasions to pay him, I never actually paid him at all for hundreds of hours of tuition. Occasionally he would remind me that the only payment he actually required was for me to "get it right". If these qualities do not smack of greatness, then I don't know what do.

This is the reason I believe that this book is completely different from many other sources on the subject of singing. It is really about the process of transformation, our perceptions of ourselves and our relationship to our environment and the universe. It uses the singing process in a completely unique way as a vehicle of transportation.

Having now studied and sung alongside a vast range of people, ranging from top professionals to young children from a wide range of backgrounds, I feel I have been provided with the richest of experiences, which now enables me to engage with individuals and the art of vocalising in an insightful and empowering manner. I hope to help individuals of all ages, styles and backgrounds to understand themselves and the processes of vocal expression to the point whereby they find personal peace, a sense of fulfilment and achievement and a connectedness to something very powerful, so that they may find themselves to be more harmonious and productive for themselves and for others also.

Ashley Kirkham 2019

ACKNOWLEDGEMENTS

Immeasurable thanks to the late Dan Gregory, my singing teacher, for your patience, knowledge, humility and your relentless pursuit of the craft. Thanks also to your daughter Joy, who was always wonderfully supportive and encouraging.

Enormous thanks to my mum and dad for always loving, supporting and believing in me.

Thank you to my beautiful wife Clare and wonderful son Robert for just being.

Thanks to Johnny Marr for your open-mindedness, enthusiasm, lack of ego, humility and for the suggestion to write this book.

Thank you so much to Gwen and Wilf Jones for years of fantastic support on our shared study of song.

Thanks to John Hurst for your recognition and pursuit of the truth and your support and encouragement. Thanks particularly for your detailed literary and conceptual contributions.

Thanks to my sister Kendra, who has explored the mysteries of the universe with me.

Thanks to Ian Kelsall for exploring life's mysteries with me.

Thanks to my nephews Natham and Gareth for their enthusiasm, feedback and belief.

Thanks so much to my editor Chris Newton for his carefully-crafted editorial detail and his open-mindedness and enthusiasm to help me, and to his colleagues Toni and Ray for their marketing and artistic contributions to the project.

Thanks to my students, who allow me to keep practising the art.

WHAT THIS BOOK IS ABOUT

This book is about the craft of vocalising, with a particular reference to singing. It is not a training manual or textbook on the physiology and mechanics of the vocal process or a 'teach yourself to sing' book. It is an information book to give insight and inspiration to those who wish to explore and experience the singing process in a very natural and powerful manner. I hope it will inspire the reader to more fully appreciate the incredible tapestry of layers and pathways involved in freeing the singing process, ranging from the simple and practical through to the invisible and intangible.

The information in this book will hopefully lead

the reader towards an exploration and engagement with the knowledge contained and the consequential experiences discussed in the book. I hope also that readers who wish to explore the singing process with me in person will make contact.

HOW TO READ THIS BOOK

The book is presented in the form of short and succinct sections of text which, to a point, are independent in themselves and yet generally contribute to the book's message as a whole. I have written it in the hope that you will follow the book from start to finish as it has been written, and that you will also pause and contemplate the detail of a single section of text at times and follow any logical pathways of thought that show themselves. This format should also allow the random selection of text to still have relevance to itself, to pathways and also to the whole. In this way you will be guided to wisdom and experience as an individual, rather than being taken through a sequential textbook and training manual on the rules of singing.

Truth based on knowledge, application and experience should be revealed to you as a natural consequence of your freedom to pursue and find your own truth. The purpose of this book then is to show that the fruits of your focus are an empirical consequence of guidance through the correct pathways.

HOW THE BOOK IS STRUCTURED

To make this book effective, I have taken care to present the information so that it is as helpful as possible. The various elements are not exactly linear or sequential in nature and the starting point may not be the same for everyone. It is difficult to talk exclusively about individual aspects of singing without bringing other elements into the discussion, and it is equally difficult to discuss so many interrelated elements simultaneously without appearing over-fastidious. I have therefore opted for a logical compromise to the structure of the information and have purposely separated the process into defined areas.

The first areas under discussion concern the voice itself, whose main constituent parts are naturally divided into three mechanisms; the lungs, the vocal folds within the larynx, and the articulators. In lay terms and for the purposes of this book, these would be described as 'breath', 'sound' and 'words'.

In slightly more technical terms the lungs pump air (the fuel of the voice) and create air flow and pressure which cause the vocal cords/folds to vibrate and chop the air flow into audible pulses. The folds lie within the larynx, and the muscles of the larynx adjust their length and tension to fine-tune the pitch and tone. The articulators (the parts of the vocal tract above the larynx) articulate and filter the sound and act to influence the strength of the laryngeal air flow and in turn the strength of the sound source.

The idea then is to allow these three connected areas to express themselves as naturally and efficiently as possible without attempting to artificially manipulate them to your own ends. If you seek to artificially control the natural mechanisms of vocalising, you are likely to produce a product that is somehow limited, contrived and reduced in honesty, integrity, purity and humanity.

After a natural introduction into the journey and beyond these three elements of breath, sound and words, I will move on to matters relating to the deeper and sometimes intangible and invisible aspects of singing in the section called 'The invisible craft'. Here I will talk about mind, sensation, feelings, emotions and perceptions and then finally move on to performing and teaching. I will not spend time and effort in discussing all the many things the singer should not be doing in their singing journey, as this would provide unnecessary clutter to a book whose perspective is on great clarity and simplicity. My wish therefore for the reader is for them to assume that any information I have not included is either irrelevant or unhelpful.

Although I will make reference in the book to several areas where the singer may be in error in some form and how situations may be viewed differently, my overall aim will be to focus on what to do or think rather that the opposite, so that the book as a whole emphasises correct application of good habits that will of themselves fix the challenges that may be experienced by the singer. My teacher always used to remind me that if you are trying *not* to do something, then you are already wrong, and for this reason I am adopting this approach where possible in the book. It has served me well personally and I have found it most effective in guiding my students very quickly into a productive mindset rather than leaving them in a frustrated and negative mindset which is likely to prevent them moving forward effectively in the process.

We are all on a journey, and that journey is individual. With this in mind, this book is written for students delving for the first time into the craft of singing, those who are seeking the deeper spiritual aspects of singing as an expression of their own true selves, and also for musicians, teachers, performers, actors and anybody else who wishes to understand.

The book is written with the intention of helping as many people as possible to move forward on their journey. Ultimately the process is a human and empirical journey and it is for each person to apply logic, observation and patience in order to make a discerned and calculated choice about what they believe to be the truth. The truth about singing is already there, inside us, in perfect form – nature in action, waiting to be revealed.

The information in this book will cover and explain concepts ranging from the very straightforward to ideas which will require a deeper understanding and a willingness to step into such arenas as detachment, surrender, conscious awakening and the willingness to place oneself at the source of a creative process. The deeper awareness gained from working in this way allows the pure unfolding of the desired result.

Of course, singing cannot truly be learned just by reading a book; the written word can only ever be a reference point and a guide. Having said this, however, I wish very much for this book to be an inspirational document to inform and transform the individual. The person-to-person relationship between student and teacher is vital to guide the would-be singer from knowledge into living experience. There are far too many complexities that need to be considered when it comes to the needs of the individual, as each student will need to be carefully guided through their experiences. This process must be conducted 'live'. Once the student has then experienced singing in the context of their own individual makeup, then the process will become real to them and will no longer be just information on a page.

It is vitally important for the reader to remember this: *the best you can be is already inside you*. Unfortunately it is all wrapped up in the complexities of being who you are. So every emotion, perception, belief and paradigm will directly manifest itself into your vocal production. The task is therefore to discover how to understand yourself to such a degree whereby the singing process is revealed as a consequence of peeling away the packaging: hence the title of the book – "The Voice Revealed".

WHAT IS SINGING?

Singing itself is a type of vocal expression using words, pitches and durations. It comes under the umbrella of vocalising, which is a term used to describe any type of voice usage. We have countless words for vocal expression - talking, rapping, chanting, scatting, speaking, throat singing, saying, calling, declaiming, announcing, yelling, bellowing, exclaiming, yodelling, shouting, humming, recitative and reciting to name but a few.

Many great speech makers convey such eloquence and tone that listening to them speak feels like listening to a great operatic aria. Likewise, there are performers who deliver a song that sounds musical and intelligent and yet is more akin to speech than singing. Perhaps in vocalising it is just the imposed labels that make the divisions, and this human process of labelling can ultimately restrict and limit these natural processes, which simply require permission to express themselves as nature or the circumstances intended.

The aim of this book then is to celebrate all the stylistic diversity contained within this umbrella term 'vocalising', with a particular emphasis on looking to reveal the essential elements that underpin all singing, whatever the characteristics or style, age or gender of the performer.

WHY DO WE SING?

To some singers, the process might just be a bit of fun, to enable them to express themselves and gain confidence. To others it might be a process of spiritual and personal awakening. It is therefore important to access those aspects they feel will help them now and look to other aspects in the future if they feel impelled to do so.

Any true singer will sing because they must. It is their nature and innate desire. A singer also knows that there is something of personal significance about the act. The process of oxygenating the system enhances the well-being of the individual. The shared experience of singing with others is also another aspect of intimate communication and openness, which again can promote well-being and positive energy flow.

Some individuals sing to feed their egos or to seek adoration from others. For some the success is the journey itself. Some pursue singing because they like a particular performer or style and wish to emulate it. Others may feel they have something to aspire to, or something or someone to connect to. Some feel lacking in confidence or self-awareness and feel more comfortable pretending to become something other than themselves – akin to the confidence some people gain from acting. Some are just drawn to or are inquisitive of the whole singing phenomenon. It may be simply that they are often astounded by the sounds and feelings and emotions that are generated by singing and are intrigued enough to explore the craft further. There are times of course when we just haven't a clue why we wish to sing or why we like to watch and listen to other people sing. We simple feel impelled, inspired, moved, cleansed or rejuvenated.

WHY IS THE VOICE DIFFERENT FROM ALL OTHER INSTRUMENTS?

The obvious difference between the human voice and other instruments is that rather than being 'outside' the body, the voice is 'inside' and physically connected to everything we are, including our emotions, perceptions and physical health. A singer may find that they need to take care of what they eat, such as excessive dairy products, which can be mucus forming. Air conditioning can dry out the respiratory system, as can smoky atmospheres, too little exercise and illness. A cellist or a drummer may struggle with energy levels or concentration if they are ill, or a wind player may need to be creative with their breathing because of a blocked nose or sore throat, but their actual instrument is in perfect working order. If a singer has a throat infection, laryngitis or a bad cold or if they are upset and mentally disturbed, it can often be very difficult, if not impossible, to give a satisfactory performance.

WHAT THEN PREVENTS US FROM SINGING?

Many of the challenges a singer may face are self-created and typically include emotional limiters such as fear, doubt, anxiety and embarrassment. A difficulty for many people is that they hold so many feelings and perceptions inside them that the personal act of opening themselves up to intimate expression is often too perturbing and emotional. Obviously, bottling up emotions is not healthy either, and it can become a barrier to effective singing.

Misconceptions such as pitch being defined as 'high and low', the belief that physical breathing exercises are needed or that 'projection', 'placement' or 'covering' of the voice is required are all typical man-made attempts to entrain nature rather than allowing it to behave as it knows and wishes.

We can never control exactly what happens when we instruct our bodies to sing. In fact, the result of anything we desire cannot be directly controlled. This is because the result of anything is the consequence of controlling the conditions that create it, allowing the 'result' the freedom it needs to express itself. It is therefore essential to work out what those unique singing conditions are for 'us' and work to control them. Discovering these unique conditions will allow the resulting voice to reveal itself. Trying to control the result of anything means that in some way we are gripping, influencing or forcing the result into an unnatural place of our own will. The voice needs to be freed and it cannot be gripped and freed at the same time.

HOW IS IT ALL MEASURED?

Many of the principles discussed in this book will be

simple in nature, although 'simple' must never be confused with 'easy'. Being simple in nature does not mean that it is simple to explain using the written word. Reading about the process will only ever be useful as a motivator and informer. Certain features of singing are mechanical; they are audible and measurable, whilst other features are invisible to the physical senses and need to be perceived through empirical means – trial and error - and one-to-one guidance.

Learning to sing is a journey of discovery – discovering what works and what does not. The student must, however, never think that making an error is failure; it is merely another step closer to discovering what is right. One fundamental element must be to always replace incorrect thinking with correct thinking. If the singer's mind is focused on trying not to do something, then they are already wrong. We all develop poor habits and it is essential not to try and unlearn these habits; the emphasis must be on replacing poor habits with good habits. We will fail and grow disheartened, but the more we fail the more we will learn. It will be much more productive to develop an attitude that will see the challenges encountered as stepping stones rather than stumbling blocks.

Typically, like most learning, singing is filled with endless shifts and plateaus. The singer will battle and graft without apparent progress, then sometimes unexpectedly make a shift – then plateau again until the next shift. Strangely, shifts often occur following the most difficult struggles, so it is important to try not to demand a result but rather focus on the conditions that will reveal the results over time.

WHERE DO I START?

Before moving on to the singing journey, it is important to think carefully where you are at this moment in time. What attributes do you already possess naturally, and what areas do you feel need developing? Being a singer is not just about voice. Presence, personality, musicality, intelligence, energy, stillness, warmth, vitality, integrity, honesty, physiology, knowledge, experience, physical attraction and courage all play their part. So it is most important to firstly gain a perspective on where you are now, so that a strategy can be developed to plan for where you would like to be in the future.

Talents and skills are attributes that need to be evaluated early in the vocalising process as part of mapping your own makeup. Talents are of course abilities possessed naturally, whereas skills are abilities that are learned. Potential, up to a point, is unknown. This is a difficult area to assess so early in your journey, but because you may feel that you may be less talented vocally than you would like, there are other qualities that go towards creating an accomplished performer.

HOW THEN DO WE TRANSFORM OURSELVES?

The transformational aspect of the process is different for each individual and is typically based on several aspects. These include an individual's ability to perceive their own state of conscious presence or inner being - Whether they are conscious of this or not - natural abilities and talents already present such as good tone quality, a good range or a natural sense of communication with an audience, and also the number and types of preconceptions, misunderstandings and blocks that may also be present within them. These might include shyness, lack of confidence, embarrassment, a tendency to over-control key elements of singing, consciously reaching mentally and physically for high notes, or perhaps working too hard physically to control the breathing process.

Much of the time, in order to free the voice, we first need to learn to free ourselves. Each time one small aspect of the process is perceived in a different light, a little bit more of a transformation affecting the whole individual will take place.

A simple analogy for this transformation would be the act of walking briskly up a flight of stairs. If you were to first walk with the thought of lifting your feet one at a time to ascend each step, and then perform the same act whilst thinking of putting your feet down for each step, you would find that the mere change of thinking for each event would produce an entirely different experience. This book will work in much the same way. If a number of aspects of the process can be altered to create a more insightful, efficient, freeing and enjoyable process, then it will be likely to have a cumulative and transformation affect overall.

2

BREATH

A fundamental understanding of breathing is essential in singing, as air is the principal vehicle for transporting sound and helps to oxygenate the body and enliven the senses. Breathing in singing should be as natural a process as breathing in speaking.

WHY DO WE SOMETIMES STRUGGLE TO BREATHE EFFECTIVELY?

One reason a singer may struggle to breathe effectively in singing is because they may think of speaking and singing as very different activities. Once they discover that they are very similar, they will then find that their singing breath becomes as natural as their speaking breath.

BREATH AND POSTURE

An ideal posture for singing is to see with your mind's eye an imaginary cord lifting you up from the centre of the top of your head. If you perceive this correctly, your body will feel a natural 'lift' with the frame of the body raised by a thought, allowing the muscles to hang in a relaxed manner over the frame of the body, much like a garment hanging elegantly from a hanger.

Information can however only guide you towards good breathing, for it is only when you experience effective breathing for yourself that you will really understand. Explanations often only have meaning when they are tied to an experience. We can be told what an apple looks like and tastes like, but we need to taste it for ourselves to truly know.

BREATHING MECHANICS

Most breath should be conducted with the mouth open. This allows the maximum amount of air to be exchanged in the most efficient manner as part of the singing process. It should also be as noiseless as possible.

There is no need whatsoever to have an involvement with the physical breathing exercises promoted by many singers and singing teachers, which typically involve pushing and tucking in stomach muscles, relaxing shoulders and trying to mechanically control the workings of the diaphragm etc. Much of this will just lead to physical tension and frustration and is nowhere near as effective as breath which naturally occurs as a consequence of understanding both the obvious and the more subtle but powerful mechanisms of the craft.

THE BREATH OF ANTICIPATION

It is vital to breathe with the same feel, focus and attention you would normally and naturally apply in speech, ensuring that the breath before a phrase is a natural breath of anticipation for the phrase ahead, incorporating the knowledge and intention of exactly what you wish to impart. In this way the audience will be drawn to engage in your intentions and perceptions before you even sing a note.

PERCEIVED PROBLEMS

It is nearly always something other than the breath that makes a singer believe he or she has a breathing problem. Poor vocal tone, which often uses more breath than it should, is often tackled through attempts to improve the breathing process rather than fixing the quality of the tone, which will of itself lead to using less breath.

There should never be any requirement for a singer to take an abnormally large breath. There is sufficient air in a normal pair of lungs to fuel all parts of a song. What is paramount is that this air is used efficiently.

Poor use of breath by the singer may reveal itself through breathing at inappropriate times or fulfilling the singer's own unintentional self-fulfilling prophecy that they believe that they will run out of breath; because they believe it, they do so.

It may be that the singer is trying to take enormous breaths for the perceived singing effort ahead and causing themselves unnecessary physical tension. It may be that instead of trying to take a breath, they should instead be taking an audible pause that implies a breath or break in time.

The singer may be taking breaths at the wrong time, setting up a domino effect of other awkward breathing choices as a consequence. They may be adding breathing qualities to words that do not need them such as singing 'hyou' instead of 'you', or they might be exhaling at the cessation of the sound, leaving themselves with a quick panicked catch-up breath before the next phrase.

It is often good practice to take subtle liberties with the duration of certain notes; to augment or diminish the length of them to allow more time for a desired breath, time to put in a soft glottal and time to allow a more powerful accentuation of a particular word. It can sometimes be a little like jazz, where the performer adds a little and takes a way a little here and there but overall stays with the durations required.

BREATH WITHOUT VOICE

A singer is still performing even though they may not be vocalising at all times. In effect this means that for a proportion of time the singer is dealing with various types of performed silence; an interesting concept indeed.

When singers perform silences which lie in between sung phrases, they will typically be breathing silently in one of four different ways; a *preparation breath* or *breath of anticipation,* which is taken before a sung phrase has begun, the *quick breath* or *planned breath* which occurs in between sung phrases, the *finishing breath* which follows the audible cessation of the sound and the *normal breath* which occurs during extended periods of silence. Once you appreciate this, you will be aware of these subtleties in your performing and should now give them some consideration as you plan the delivery of your song to an audience.

BREATH WITH VOICE

For breath *with* the voice, careful consideration needs to be given to the relationship between tone quality and the breath. As it is often poor tone quality that makes a singer run out of breath during a phrase, the singer may assume that a poor preparatory breath has caused the problem. Therein lies the assumption that the singer needs to create an artificially augmented breath prior to vocalising.

The simple truth is that for most musical phrases

there is already sufficient breath in the lungs. It is so often the inefficient use of that breath that is the real issue. For this reason, if the singer feels they are struggling to sustain a phrase, they may well benefit from looking to the quality of their vocal tone as a first port of call. The likelihood will be that they are using too much breath. Fixing or improving the tone will often fix or improve the breath usage.

Tone quality is not just a matter of a good round sound; it is much more to do with the appropriateness of the tone. The appropriate tone is produced when the mind of the performer is focused on the emotion or meaning associated with a word or phrase. The appropriate tone is not deliberately produced by the singer but is the natural product of the performer's intention at source. Meaning is not put into words, but is allowed to reveal itself.

When a person is angry, do they think to themselves: "I am going to produce an angry tone" and then take a consciously different breath before their rant? No; they have a reason for their anger, and angry tone is produced as a consequence. When a person laughs, they do not take a consciously appropriate breath before deliberately producing a planned laughter tone.

Nature works in a very straightforward manner. There is an intention which produces a result of its own volition. If the focus of attention for the singer is on the source of the creative process, be it a meaning or emotion or a word, then there is no need to be concerned with the appropriate breath or tone quality, because that will naturally and consequentially produce itself.

Many books on spiritual or universal law from ancient and modern text emphasise detachment from our desires and a focus on our intentions. With this in mind, it is well worth spending time making a conscious note of the tone quality produced by people we observe, but with a particular focus on the person's intention. Notice whether they are angry, laughing or depressed, then notice that their voice quality and delivery changes in accordance with their focus and presence of mind.

BREATH AND MIND

The individual's perception of breath and mind is often a vital factor in singing, as the breath will be directly influenced by what the mind believes is true. If the singer only focuses mentally on a word at a time, they will be unlikely to sing the required phrases musically. To be fully effective, the mind needs to encompass the meaning of the song as a whole prior to any utterance, the meaning of each word as it is absorbed at each moment in time, the meaning of each phrase, and the singer must also be conscious of what is going to be said next, and what will follow that.

With the mind focused in this way, the breath automatically fits itself to the duration of the phrases to be sung. If the mind doubts whether there will be sufficient breath to accommodate the phrase, then the performer will certainly run out of breath.

On many occasions a verbal phrase may be physically broken into segments as part of a piece, and it is vital that the singer keeps the whole phrase in mind. Failure to do so may affect continuity for the performer and audience. In this instance, the fragmented phrases must be treated using the preparatory/anticipatory breath with an accompanying sense of momentum and continuous purpose. If the singer has in their mind all complete phrases and their connectivity to each other, then the audience will also and automatically share the same experience. This is certainly why as much performing as possible should be done from memory, as this will allow the maximum focus on the narrative and its conveyance. The intimate relationship created with the audience when a soloist sings is weakened if the singer is looking at the music instead of at the audience.

BREATH AND WORDS

A prerequisite for all performers should be to start by reading the words separately from the song itself. Reading with natural weighting and intelligence without being influenced by the melodies, rhythms and harmonies that are associated with the song itself allows the performer to return to the song afresh but with the memory of just the words in their natural and raw form.

No composer should be using words in a song format unless the addition of music improves the piece or adds additional meaning or insight. If the additions do not fulfil these requirements, then the composer should leave the words to tell their story as intended by the writer.

Once you have read the words to a song and

taken time to contemplate and embed the phrases, weighting, structure, emotions and narrative, you should have gained a purer insight into the naturalness of delivery required and the breaths needed to serve the narrative.

Sometimes the performer can tell whether the words were the inspiration of a song or whether they were added to the music afterwards. Music should only be associated with words if the process adds something to one or both. Certainly a heightened awareness of the relationship between the words and music will help the singer to phrase the breathing process with more intelligence, and if the music runs against the nature of the words then the performer would need to question the composer's intention. Perhaps the piece is purposefully creative in some way, or just poorly written.

BREATH PERCEPTION

The way the mind perceives the breath is significant to the singer. In general, it is helpful to perceive the whole body breathing and not just the actual respiratory system. This will give the process a more holistic and naturally efficient feel. It cannot be just thought however: it needs to be perceived gradually over time through a process of stillness, contemplation, patience and observation.

MIND AND BREATH

Although the mind's perception of breath has a direct effect upon the management of that breath, it is also very important to understand the effect that breath has upon the mind. Certain simple breathing exercises can significantly assist in stilling and calming the mind prior to and after singing. The point of stillness within the singer can be strengthened when breathing and counting are performed in a calculated and balanced manner. The act of regulating these two elements causes the mind itself to become more balanced and centred. This in turn creates ideal conditions for the singer's task.

There are many variations of nose, mouth and nostril breathing techniques including a variety of different ratios of inhalations, exhalations, pausing and held breaths. These various types of breathing will not be discussed in any detail in this book, but cause degrees of stillness, focus, lightness, calm and clarity. Exploration and practice of some of these techniques will help any performer stay balanced and clear in thought.

An unusual but effective breathing technique that may be used outside the performance arena would be the closing of the eyes, stillness of body and the watching of the breath. This exercise can create a wonderful sense of deep calm once the initial strangeness has settled. The idea is to merely watch the breath in and out whilst making no conscious effort to affect the process. It may feel as though the breath is never going to take itself, but eventually it does, and gradually it becomes more and more natural, deep and calming.

3

SOUND

A singer's sound should be free, natural and honest and should reveal its acoustic comfort with a natural resonance. The tone should be appropriate to the purpose of the song as a direct consequence of the singer's perception of the intention and meaning at source, allowing the perception's conveyance through delivery.

To artificially put meaning into words and sound is to create a substandard article. The meaning and intention must merely be observed within the performer, allowing the meaning that lies within the words or intention to be naturally conveyed as a consequence of a true, honest and immovable perception at source.

Any misconceptions by the performer that run contrary to delivery of the purpose or intention of the singing will inevitably deliver an inferior product. It is therefore your role as a singer to understand the craft of singing to such a degree that whatever you commit, omit or perceive allows the singing the freedom it needs to express itself fully.

To 'allow the singing its freedom' means understanding yourself to the point where you perceive the singing looking after itself, simply by 'getting out of the way'. It is human nature of course for the individual to think they know better than nature and rather than trusting nature, often decide to try to control it for themselves. Therefore, much of the practice required by the singer is concerned with ascertaining what they are, and are not, allowing to happen.

REGISTER

Register is the range of notes experienced by the individual as they access what are conventionally termed lower, medium and higher pitches. These are sensations often termed 'chest voice', 'middle voice' and 'head voice' and are the *consequence* of good singing and not the *cause*. One might sense more chest resonance when singing 'lower' notes, but this does not mean that the singer should always focus on the chest area to produce the desired tone in the lower range. These are the resonances selected naturally by your inner acoustic intelligence once you have allowed the conditions for good vocalising to prevail.

To focus on enhancing sound by intentionally giving it more chest, nose or cheek emphasis for example, will only cause an imbalance of tonal quality, and it might make you focus more on making an impressive sound than conveying the meaning of a song. If you focus on the sound rather than its meaning, so will the audience, and the all-important message and emotions conveyed by the song will be compromised or lost.

Any attempt by the singer to control and manipulate the desired vocal result will often mean that the source that creates it has been bypassed or subordinated. In a nutshell, the ego, given the chance, will observe a consequence of natural acoustic function and will then seek to artificially control it rather than allowing it to happen as a direct consequence of perception at the source. Unfortunately, the singer can never make a result happen by controlling it. Singers can only create the conditions which increase the likelihood of the desired result occurring.

Although the focus on the source of the creative process of vocalising may seem simplistic, it only mirrors what we experience in much of our lives as universal law. This approach to much of the singing craft also reminds us that our focus on the journey will of itself increase our likelihood of achieving our desired goals. Any excessive focus on the desired result may potentially increase the likelihood of losing awareness of the entire creative process.

Given an opportunity, the ego will try to over-analyse and manipulate nature and will cause vocalising to become limited or contrived – not at all what the singer really wants.

We all have a natural in-built facility for producing exact pitches and tone quality. If we can place ourselves as close as we can to the right conditions, then the correct vocal tone and delivery will manifest themselves. If, however, we seek to artificially create the desired tone and its delivery by bypassing our own intentions, we are likely to be interfering unhelpfully with our own ability to manifest the appropriate result.

PITCH

Pitch for singers is a concept that needs to be thought of differently from the way it is applied to manufactured instruments. This is because the singer has to produce the right frequency mentally. He or she has to create an imaginary scale or ladder, or perception, of pitches in terms of height to comprehend and reproduce the different frequencies and appreciate their relationship to one another in the form of intervals. This process can be both conscious and unconscious.

Up to the point of formal written sheet music, pitch has functioned as part of an aural and oral tradition and has not needed to be written down in any constructive form. People just listened and repeated and memorised different frequencies and intervals. For an instrumental player the same mental perceptions do not have to be developed; the player needs only to learn the correct fingering, hand position, lip pressure etc. to player the required frequencies.

There did of course come a point in time where the need for writing musical information down came to the fore. As pitches are different speed vibrations, naturally interpreted by man as 'higher' and 'lower', this persuaded the original inventors of written musical symbols in Western music to place the created symbols visually higher and lower upon a framework called a stave. To a singer this concept is particularly unhelpful as it can often persuade the singer to reach, stretch and contort the body, causing strain and tension to the sound. If a singer truly believes that pitches are 'higher' and 'lower' than each other then they will be very likely to chase and try to control those pitches mentally and in turn physically.

Having said this however, the study of pitches, scales and keys will normally become a natural part of a musician's study and an integral aspect of this study will involve the automatic creation of pitches in the mind, which, as a consequence of hearing sound naturally as high and low, will inevitably involve the individual creating their own perceptions of the relationship and distance between pitches in the mind and in turn relating these perceptions to the physical production and sensations related to those mental perceptions.

Over time, individuals, groups and cultures have chosen and adopted certain pitches and groups of pitches which they feel comfortable with, make sense to them and serve a purpose. Physics and the study of musical sound have shown that there are natural acoustics occurring in nature, which have been named the 'harmonic' or 'overtone' series. This naturally produces five different pitches which interplay and harmonise naturally. This series, which we now term the 'pentatonic' scale, formed itself from the beginnings of human interaction with sound and can be found in the music of most early cultures on the planet.

All other 'scales' developed out of these natural acoustics and the various tunings of instruments that developed over time. Most of these scales contain a set number of notes and are variously and typically named 'major', 'minor', 'whole tone', 'chromatic', and 'mode', as examples.

For many singers in the Western world, the 'major' and 'minor' scales form a basis for much of the music that is created and heard. From this perspective, the 'tonic sol fah' system of pitch training for the singer provides a wonderful foundation to establish and embed an understanding of the pitch and pitch relationships associated with singing.

Tonic sol fah's 'movable doh' system allows fluid access to all pitch movement between all the variations of the major and minor principles. Created in England in the nineteenth century, it is a 'solmization' system which attributes a distinct syllable to each note of a scale. The system was variously adapted by Curwen and Kodaly in the 19th and 20th centuries respectively with the inclusion of hand signs related to the pitches in order to add a physically visual aid to the concept of pitching and pitch relationships.

An additional and beneficial consequence of the sol fah system is the awareness gained for the singer with regard to finding and pitching notes and intervals as a natural part of studying a piece and an added appreciation of harmonies and harmonising. The piano keyboard is another instrument which links happily with the tonic sol fah system to aid the visualisation and comprehension of the relationship between notes and the perceived shapes and positions of notes in chords.

In nature, and in the course of natural everyday voice usage, however, we produce the appropriate pitches as a natural consequence of our focus of mind. When we speak or shout or cry, the appropriate pitch according to acoustic law and our state of mind at that moment in time is automatically produced. The mind knows its own body and as we have relinquished our desire to control the resulting sound and pitches, then our physiology behaves according to its nature and produces the correct pitch and tone with relative ease.

If the vocalist's focus is on the conditions that create the respective pitched notes and not on the pitch of the note with regard to its 'height', they are much more likely to achieve the sound quality they desire, with its accompanying freedom of production. Of course, as a singer, most of the pitches in a song are defined, as are the durations; in natural speech they are not. The point is, however, to view the pitched notes as different frequencies and not according to their 'height'.

If the singer's mind perceives pitches as higher or lower, then every time they sing, their mind or an aspect of it will be dwelling on this fact. As a consequence, they may well 'reach' or 'stretch' for the notes and the vocal production might tighten, squeeze, crack or shout. The result of the singer following the perceived rise and fall of the pitches is often a physical manifestation. The body lifts and drops as the mind follows the pitches up and down. The shoulders may rise, the eyes might look up or the chin drop down as if to encourage the perceived higher and lower sounds respectively.

It is a fascinating exercise to monitor the use of vocal pitch when people are street selling, acting, calling to a friend, laughing, teaching etc. When people do these things, they are generally unconscious of the craft they are employing. The wonderful ringing tones they produce and their utter freedom of vocal production is a direct consequence of a focus on something other than the pitch of the sound, which is why it is produced with effortless freedom.

When listening to the programme sellers at a football match, or to the swimming instructor comfortably ringing out top B flats and high Cs, you can appreciate how their focus on their role completely frees the vocal process. Put the same people on the spot and ask them to sing the same sounds to order and you can bet your bottom dollar they will make a hash of it. This is simply because their focus of attention has changed. One focus frees the voice and the other limits it.

For the popular modern performer, the facility of 'autotune', whereby inaccurately performed pitches from the singer are artificially manipulated and corrected by technology, is unfortunately a facility that masks a singer's issues rather than solves them. Far better to discover how to allow the pitching to become improved through analysis, study and application than to become embroiled in a process that can only provide a crutch for the singer upon which they are likely to become more and more dependent.

PASSAGIO

This is another crucial concept which can be executed successfully or unsuccessfully, dependent on the understanding applied to it. It is a passage or bridge between the 'registers' of the voice. It is experienced by a singer as they move from one set of pitches which contain a similar vibratory pattern to an adjacent and different set of notes and vibratory patterns. The sensation feels awkward and tight as if the voice is going to break and often the singer will grip the sound to try and contain it rather than let it move seamlessly and naturally, which is the ideal.

As the voice moves between different pitches, the vowel shapes automatically alter as part of the acoustic and physical characteristics of the individual's anatomy and the laws of nature. This change, known as 'passagio', is most keenly felt within the small group of notes on the transitions or bridges between what is termed the 'head', 'middle' and 'chest' registers, where the consequential body vibrations and resonances are typically felt. When vocalising is performed other than in singing we are not generally aware of passagio as nature normally accommodates adjustments as necessary. These natural adjustments typically involve the alteration of vowel shapes and the space in the back of the throat.

When a person concentrates specifically on the passagio itself because he or she is preoccupied with the defined pitches of singing, it is in the mind's nature to try to control the process artificially. What the mind then does is to make judgements and measurements about what it believes is happening and create a framework with boundaries and rules, which it then seeks to impose. These typically involve artificially altering the vowel similarly to nature.

By seeking to artificially manipulate events in this way, however, the mind is sending a message to nature to say "I believe I can control things for myself". In fact it may be able to, up to a point, but it will always, in the end, fall short of the way nature would do it. This preoccupation of the individual with control will only serve to create a somewhat substandard article which may well allow the performer to assert a measure of control over circumstances, but will never really allow the full creative tapestry of expressive complexity and variety that the inner nature would wish to express.

The nature of wanting to control results is to try to limit and contain the result within a 'box' of some form. The desired result can therefore never be as free as nature intended. To seek to control a result is to lessen, minimise or reduce the thing itself in some form.

In vocalising, if there is a powerful and internal focus on an open throat with the soft palate raised and the root of the tongue lowered and the singer focused on the words and their meaning, then the individual will have the conditions he or she needs for their inner intelligence to modify the vowel shapes required naturally.

The aim then is to control the *conditions* that will allow our inner intelligence to control the voice through the frequency range that is right for us. This is not to say that this will ever be an easy thing to achieve, but through appropriate practice it will become habitual and a great deal easier. The performer ceases to chase the notes in the same way, with the result that they focus on the source or creative conditions instead of the process and allow nature to perform with much greater ease.

So, for the passagio, if the individual insists on focusing on 'pitch' as being 'high' and 'low', then they will seek to control the voice, and the passagio *will* be a challenge to be controlled or battled with. Change the focus on to the open throat and the issues surrounded the passagio will be much more naturally accommodated.

POSTURE

Just as the body of a cello amplifies the sound created by the strings, the human body is a means of amplification for the voice. If it is bent, twisted or crumpled in any way or if the air pathways are restricted, then the amplification process may well have to work harder to achieve its aim. This is not always possible on stage and some compromises do have to be made, but as a general principle it is preferable to try to keep airways and body positions natural and supported. For the amplified singer, microphone technique and adjusted volume levels can accommodate awkward body postures, but for the acoustic singer who needs to maximise audibility without the aid of technology, a more limited range of supportive body postures will be best for the individual as a rule.

In general, the body weight for the efficient singer should be on the balls of the feet with the spine straight, but without tension and with a feeling of buoyancy and uplifting. Rather than physically and consciously lifting and expanding the physique however, it is often better to use images which will naturally lift the body for the individual without the accompanying tension normally associated with a consciously physical lift.

Certain images can often be powerful in achieving a natural physical lift to the body, such as imagining a chord attached to the top of the head, pulling gently upwards. The singer should feel a natural straightening of the back, a pulling in of the tummy and a tall and proud stance. Many physical acts can be made easier by applying an image or thought in this way.

VISUALISATION

Although images can assist the singing process, *how* they are used and how they are used *in combination* is a matter for the advanced teacher. How these images are perceived and used by the singer becomes a very refined process and it is the teacher's job to assess the singer's thinking and not their singing. My teacher would constantly say to me "I am not teaching you to sing; I am teaching you to *think* sing", "You sing with a *think* and not with a *do*".

The whole process of imagery teaches the individual to see with much greater clarity; what really 'is' as opposed to what they *think* 'is'. My teacher would often tell me "it's not what you think you are, it's what you *think,* you *are*". I experienced a similar concept with a professional artist who gave me lessons for several months. His most important saying to me was "Draw what you see and not what you think you see".

The crucial point with all this imagery is not to imagine the images but to 'see' them with the mind's eye from the self, using the conscious thinking mind, and then singing with that perception. Of course, the final process of refined singing is not meant to be overkilled with an overabundance of imagery that could hinder the singing process. The various images are used as and when necessary to lead the self to its mental parking place. Once there, the images become unnecessary, as the singer is merely in a state of seeing themselves sing. It is only when the conscious mind is drawn to try and control the result that the individual can then use the appropriate imagery to lead themselves back to the self. When they become accomplished, they utilise select images that work best for them and with just a moment's focus on one or two images; then they are back where they should be. When the singer becomes very proficient, they don't even need the images. They don't even *go* there; they just *are* there.

RESONANCE

Good resonance is an essential requirement for good singing and typically feels like effortless sound-making. The mind and body seem coordinated and the physiology feels relaxed and free. To the observer the singer will seem serene and the sound seems to emanate effortlessly, without distortion or strain. For a singer, resonance occurs when the various general resonators in the body are functioning in accordance with natural acoustic law. If the back of the throat is open with the soft palate raised and the root of the tongue lowered, then the air and sound waves are free to access all the relevant resonators they choose.

The sound will have a clear pulsating quality to it. It will sound unique.

Faults experienced by the singer when these conditions are not present typically include a sense of an audible oscillation between two pitches in the form of a 'wobble' or 'vibrato'. A faster oscillation, where the sound is experienced more as a rapid reiteration of a single pitch, is sometimes termed a 'warble'.

'Tremolo' and 'vibrato' are two other words singers sometimes use to define the sound of the voice, but often inaccurately. As resonance describes the pulsating quality of a single pitched sound or a single heard sound made up from several resonating bodies, tremolo in singing describes a fluctuation in pitch from one pitch to another and back again in rapid succession, or the rapid reiteration of a single pitch. Vibrato, although desirable in some instruments, such as flute or violin, is in fact undesirable for the singer and describes an oscillatory effect produced by a fluctuation in breath pressure or pitch. This effect can be used for dramatic effect, or it may be a vocal fault caused by poor technique, overuse, fatigue or damage.

There are obvious similarities between resonance, vibrato, wobble and warble, but for the singer the pursuit of resonance is the key aim and constitutes the individual's most natural and honest sound according to the acoustic characteristics of the individual. It does take time and experience to appraise vocal sound effectively and to tell the difference between a poor-quality voice and a voice that has not yet maximised its potential for resonance. Only study, application and time will give you these skills.

The quality of a voice may be poor because it is damaged temporarily or permanently, possibly through overuse, the development of inflammation, an infection, vocal fold nodules or permanent hearing loss that may inhibit the singer's ability to produce the correct sound effectively. To a point these physical conditions will produce a poor-quality voice that may not be fixable as opposed to one that has yet to be improved through the application of the techniques and knowledge presented in this book.

Scientifically, resonance takes place when two or more bodies are vibrating at the same or related frequencies: one vibrating body causes the other to vibrate in tune with it. The first body is deemed the vibrator and the secondary bodies resonators. Resonance occurs via vibrations between touching bodies or transmitted through the air. In singing both types occur, and the transmitting bodies include the bones, cartilages and muscles of the neck, head and upper chest. Although these may not contribute much to the external sound, they do however provide a good sensation guide for the singer.

OPEN THROAT

Good singing sensations can provide evidence for the singer that his or her vocal folds are forming strong primary vibrations that are being carried to the relevant resonators. The most important resonator for the singer is the pharynx, followed by the oral cavity and the nasal cavity. The pharynx is important because it is the first cavity of any real size through which the product of the laryngeal vibrator passes. The cavities following the pharynx can only accept what it passes on. This is the reason why an 'open throat' is a prerequisite to good singing. This should be achieved *all* the time.

Initially the singer may wish to begin thinking of the singing process like a back of the throat yawn or imagine constantly drinking the sound or even imagining they are pronouncing the words with their ears. Some singers may prefer to think about the feeling of the jaw opening at the hinge or the sound being directed out of the back of the throat at the rear of the head. Of course, these images may well seem very strange at first and are merely tools or techniques which, when perceived clearly by the singer, can cause the throat to open and remain open.

An open throat is of particular relevance to very quiet singing. Often the singer will automatically feel that they will need to assert more control over this type of vocalising in order to ensure that the sound is stable, particularly during high and sustained sounds. The same huge effort to keep and sustain an open throat is the key, as both loud and quiet singing should be the same 'size', although not the same volume. If high and soft singing is gripped and over-controlled, it can so easily produce a 'small', reduced delivery. All singing, regardless of its volume, should always have 'size'.

It is vital to try and achieve this constant open throat for all vowels and consonants. The open throat acts like a doorway into all potential resonance, so that your body is always 'set up' for whatever resonance is required at any given moment. This allows the whole vocal tract a constant and clear passage. If the singer does not provide the open throat, they may well be taking away the choices of resonance the mind and body want to access. The focus of the mind's eye in the throat area is vital as a constant and immovable presence, as it causes the throat to open fully much more consistently. If the focus is more towards the front of the mouth and face, then the singer is more likely to gape with the mouth causing the throat itself to reduce in size.

SPEAKING

Speaking is a *natural* combination of voice, weight, pitch and duration of words. *Singing* is the same as speaking but with defined combinations of voice, weight, pitch and duration of words. It also includes multiple pitches to a syllable which is called melisma. Now although it might seem obvious to view speaking and singing as very different, in actual fact it is much more helpful and effective to view singing as a variation on speech. Once this is understood, then the singing becomes a much more natural event. If the singer believes that speaking and singing *are* very different, then of course they will be. The principle is very much a self-fulfilling prophecy. Once the singer realises that singing and speaking are remarkably similar, the singing will then be experienced as a very different phenomenon. My teacher used to describe singing as 'big speaking', and this is exactly how it should feel.

VOICE REGISTERS

In classical music, voice categories have been developed to help singers to choose pieces that are appropriate for their voice qualities. Pieces would typically be promoted in the classical or operatic medium as being high, medium or low or based upon a particular key, but while the same voice categories apply to popular singers, their music is not generally presented in the same way.

When considering voice categories, it is useful to know what qualities a voice has, as this will guide the singer towards singing the most appropriate pieces for them. A key is not always helpful, as it only indicates the set of notes a piece is based upon rather than the range of notes used or the general lie of the notes. Knowledge of an individual's vocal qualities will help them make an informed decision about the repertoire that is most likely to suit them and give fulfilment. The voice will then express its most fundamental nature more effectively.

Identifying your voice requires the recognition of four different qualities.

VOICE CATEGORIES

PITCH

The first quality to consider is the number of frequencies (pitches) the singer is able to sing. These form what we call a *range* of notes. The distance from the 'highest' to the 'lowest' is called the *compass*. This range and compass will categorise the performer as a *high, medium* or *low-pitched* singer. In classical music further labels would be attached corresponding to these high, medium and low ranges. For the male voice they would be tenor, baritone and bass, and for the female voices, soprano, mezzosoprano and contralto respectively.

As singing develops in an individual, they may find that their range and compass shifts a little. This is quite normal as the voice seeks its natural level. If the singer does not yet possess the ability to produce the full range of notes they feel they are potentially capable of, then it will be more difficult for them to assess their voice type for the present. Fortunately, it is not the deciding factor when categorising a voice but one of four measuring tools. It is also very important to remember that these categories are guides and are not meant to 'pigeon-hole' or limit an individual in any way.

The normal ranges of these voices are roughly one octave above and below the E, G and A below middle C for the male voices and one octave above and below the E, G and B above middle C for the female voices. The E, G and A refer to bass, baritone and tenor respectively, and the E, G and B for contralto, mezzo and soprano respectively. Many voices of course often exceed these ranges, which is why the measurement of range and compass is merely one of four indicators for voice categorisation.

Weight

The second point to consider in defining the character of your voice is its *weight*. This may indicate how agile your voice might be. The weightier voices tend to move less easily than lighter voices.

Timbre

The third consideration of voice quality in voice identification is the *colour (timbre)* of the voice. This is its characteristic texture or tone. On one side we might describe a voice in terms of light, smooth, lyrical, soft or delicate. On the other side it might be said to be rugged, robust, hard, dark, rich or full. In classical circles, there are many variations of the basic six voice categories as a direct consequence of these many variations beyond the basic range and compass.

Size

The fourth point to consider in voice categorisation is the natural 'size' of the voice, literally its volume. Of course, if the singer has not yet learned to use the full potential size of their voice, then this may be something they may need to delay judgement on.

Variations

Now consideration has been given to the four different aspects of the voice, the whole process of categorisation begins to become very creative, encompassing different roles and styles. Each category becomes subdivided and specifically described. With each subcategory one or more of these four identifying features is altered, describing the voice as perhaps more dramatic, heavier, lighter, darker, more lyrical, higher, lower, more flexible, soulful, pure etc.

Once the individual has assessed the four main qualities of voice according to range, weight, colour and size, they will need to consider the type of music that suits their four qualities and the type of music they enjoy singing. If they can manage to reach a satisfactory compromise between these elements, they will be better able to maximise the likelihood of success and fulfilment in singing.

Imitation

Although it is human nature to be inspired by other people, it can be a danger for any singer who intentionally or unintentionally copies or mimics the vocal production and delivery of another performer. If the imitating becomes too pronounced and embedded, it might be very difficult for that individual to find their own true voice. Even the sensations of sound production experienced by one person may be very different from those of another attempting to achieve the same characteristic sounds, because physically we are all unique. Much better to attempt to convey the desired qualities of another whilst allowing the result to express itself from our own unique makeup.

4

WORDS

The singer has an added dimension of complexity that other instrumentalists do not – the addition of words. What a wonderful but complex issue. It is the singer's task to simultaneously combine several forms of communication. These include expression and emotion, which of themselves are invisible at source and yet may be observed and sensed and felt by the performing individual and the audience; body language, which is physical and visual and may be conscious and unconscious; the audible language of sound; and words, which are written and audible constructs attached to vocal shapes and articulations.

VOWELS

Vowels should be the predominant vehicle of transportation for vocal sound. A vowel is created when a vocal sound is made with the mouth and vocal tract open. The vowels change their shape as the internal area of the mouth changes its shape. You can sample this movement from one vowel to another by pronouncing the phrase "Who would know aught of art must learn and then take his ease". Pronouncing the words without the consonants provides an even greater appreciation of how the vowel shapes gradually alter their shape.

Vowels require ample space to be effective, and an open throat is a prerequisite to this end. A raised soft palate and the root of the tongue lowered will provide this space. Mental images can be used to ensure the open throat, which require practice in visualisation techniques and are essential for keeping the mind focused on the task. A 'yawn' is a typically good image to use for all open throat singing.

DIPHTHONGS

In many words there is a movement from one vowel to

another, which is called a 'diphthong'. The word 'how' looks like a simple monosyllable, but in reality it contains a diphthong which consists of an 'ah' sound moving to an 'ooh' sound. To preserve the optimum space for the singer, the emphasis must be on maintaining the first vowel for as long as possible, as it is normally a more open sound than the second. Where this is not the case, then the singer may need to decide which vowel to give priority to, or even use a 'hybrid' between the two. Awareness and the appropriate application of the diphthong will enhance the singer's ability to sustain a musical phrase with much greater ease, particularly long phrases. The singer may often need to explore the feeling of an open and closed sound as the voice moves between different frequencies and different word shapes and durations.

CONSONANTS

When the lips, tongue, throat and teeth temporarily stop or obstruct the flow of a vowel, it is called a consonant. Consonants may be used before, during or after vowels and help to define the meaning of a word. They may be voiced or unvoiced. For singers it is vital to utilise this vowel, diphthong and consonant relationship with simplicity and intelligence in order to maximise the meaning that lies within the words. Consonants should interfere as little as possible with the creation of space, but they of course do so, as it is their nature. It is therefore the singer's job to articulate only as much as is necessary and allow the vowels and diphthongs as much time as possible.

GLOTTALS

The 'glottal stop' is a vital feature of speech and word usage that is often greatly underestimated and very under-used. It comes mainly in two forms, soft and hard, and occurs when the there is a space between the vocal cords or 'folds'. In singing it shows itself predominantly at the beginning of words such as 'ear' or 'arm' where the closing and opening of the glottis is accompanied by a release of air. It often precedes a vowel and helps to clearly define a word. Unfortunately, many performers develop the very poor habit of carrying over the ending consonant of a previous word and in so doing, unintentionally fail to use the glottal. This of course affects the overall meaning and communicative requirements for effective conveyance of the narrative. To quote an example, "Hold you in my arms" becomes "hold you win ma yarms".

PRONUNCIATION

The focus for the effective production of all vowels and accompanying articulations should be the centre of the self, where the mind's eye can see the words clearly. From this vantage point it is difficult to mispronounce words, as the mind produces the appropriate result in response to that which it perceives.

If the individual's attention is in the front of the face and mouth area, then the sound is likely to be more nasal and consonants will typically be over emphasised or double-sounded, so an 'm' sound might typically be sounded 'mm m'. It is as though you are saying mm-mat instead of mat.

If the 'm' sound is perceived with the mind's eye at a point in between the ears or at the root of the tongue whilst simultaneously perceiving that word in the mind, then the 'm' will be performed efficiently and move immediately on to the vowel. By perceiving all vowels, consonants, diphthongs and breath at this very place in the mind, you will place the source of all singing at the point of the open throat and therefore maximise full and appropriate resonance and encourage yourself to anchor your inward gaze effectively.

An individual cannot relax the focus from its point between the ears or the root of the tongue for a single moment if he or she wishes to be effective. This is because the mind, through habit and belief, will seek to move the perception of the consonant from this position of stillness and try to mentally pronounce the words at the physical point of articulation in the mouth area. What the mind perceives is real and has real and audible consequences.

Although focusing the mind's eye's attention on word pronunciation at the site of the open throat may initially seem strange, it is helpful to remind ourselves that there are a great many functions of everyday life which when studied more closely are only variations of the same. Take for example the practice of reading silently from a book or silently spelling words and letters out in our minds as we type on a keyboard. If we actually observe the process, we will find that we are forming, shaping, articulating and pronouncing the words in our minds as if we were moving something to pronounce these sounds, and yet no physical movement is present at all, even though it feels as though we are forming and saying the words.

Observe somebody who is depressed and you will tend to find that their attention and focus has moved to the front of the face and that their words and delivery may appear nasal, mumbled and unclear.

A few simple exercises to illustrate effective and ineffective focus on pronunciation will suffice to illustrate the result of the correct and incorrect focus of mind. Where the mind is focussed, and how it sees the words, will dictate the resulting pronunciation. I will explain it here with the correct pronunciation first followed by the typically incorrect pronunciation afterwards. 'your eyes' becomes 'your reyes', 'told you' becomes 'tol joo', I want you' becomes 'I wan choo', 'for ever' becomes 'for-rever' and 'and I' becomes 'an di'.

It is in the singer's interest to maximise the potential that lies within a vowel, as it is the means by which vocal sound is most freely expressed. The articulated consonant temporarily or permanently obstructs the vowel and should be given just enough consideration to define the respective word before giving attention back to the vowel. The diphthong must be given due attention to maximise space of the first vowel, as closing onto a vowel with less natural space will often limit the singer's ability to sustain and allow the effective shaping of a vocal phrase. In fact, with a bigger emphasis on vowels and with the direction of thought focused securely inwards, it becomes more and more natural for consonants to occur of their own volition. It seems a strange concept to convey, but when the mind's eye perceives a specific location for production of a word, it is then nature's natural solution to produce the consequential result in speech. The mind is ever the builder. It creates out of thought and automatically allows production of what it perceives.

Good and predictable diction will always be helpful to the audience, as they will use less energy and focus trying to decipher what the singer is saying. If the diction is poor, the audience may struggle to understand the meaning of the words and, as a consequence, will be engaging in the piece as a whole to a lesser degree.

A typical phrase from a song such as "hold you in my arms" can, unbelievably, be broken into a mixture of fifteen consonant and vowel sounds; H, oh, ooh, l, d, y, ooh, ih, n, m, a, ee, ah, m and z. If any of these fifteen sounds and shapes are unduly altered or replaced, this will automatically affect the meaning and may consciously or unconsciously draw the audience's attention away from the purpose of the song. This is because people use an automatically predictive approach to words and phrases they hear based on their experience of similar and familiar phrases from the past. Having heard the first few words of a familiar phrase or sentence, they will guess what is coming next. If for example the first part of a phrase is "I love you so", then the observer would already be assuming that the next words will be "much", or "never leave me", or "don't leave me" and so on. If at any point in the line the audience hears an unexpected or unfamiliar phrase, or one that is not easily recognised because it has been mispronounced, they will be distracted and will try to work out what is being said. As a result of this they may then partially lose the thread of a song or other elements of a song.

As an example, "hold you in my arms" may typically be mispronounced in a number of ways. 'Hold you' may be altered to 'hol ju','hoh ju', 'hohoo ju' or 'hohool ju', or 'my arms' to 'ma yarms' or even missing off the final 'ms' completely. 'You in' might typically be changed to 'you win'. Sustaining the 'n' sound in the word 'in' and the 'm' sound in 'my' and 'arms'; This would be an example of unintentionally using nasal consonants as vowels. Two final and typical mispronunciations from just this one phrase are 'my' as 'mayee' and missing the 'h' sound or the final 'd' from 'hold'.

If a singer unduly alters most phrases of a song in such a manner, then one can easily imagine the clarity of the song's meaning becoming more and more blurred.

WEIGHTING

If we were robots without emotion and expression, we would deliver every word in the same manner and with the same speed and weight. Every syllable would be delivered like a monosyllabic pulse, devoid of humanity. We as humans would find this manner stifling, as we comprehend the meaning of words to a large extent through our understanding of intention based on our response to feelings and experiences. Because of these experiences and our innate desire to communicate we have naturally developed *weighting*, whereby we emphasise or flavour words to convey their meaning more strongly.

Weighting is not something we do for its own sake; it is more the result of our understanding of words and our experience in maximising their communicative potential. Through our additional understanding of how the natural rhythm of words adheres to an ever-changing pulse, when we use words, we impart an endless variety of different weightings to them, to focus the listener on the words we feel are *more* important and less weighting to those we feel have less importance. We often pause, or slow down, or speed up, or lengthen or shorten words or phrases in our attempt to communicate effectively.

If the words of a song are important and need to be understood effectively, then it is vital for the singer to give the natural weighting of the words priority over other considerations such as the melody. If the singer focuses their mind on the rise and fall of the melody, then they are likely to give less importance to the natural communicative potential of the weighting of the words. Of course, if the words are less important, they may be latched on to the melody with a sometimes-unnatural weighting. It of course depends on how well the words and melody have been set together. The singer will need to decide at any given moment in time, but certainly the weighting of the words and the pitch will always be vying for attention, with the result being a consequence of this relationship and the perception and intention of the performer, lyricist and composer combined.

WORDS

Before engaging in any song, I advise to always make a habit of reading the words or lyrics separately from the melodic and rhythmical influence of a song to ascertain its natural weighting and rhythm according to speech. Then attach it back to the pitches of the melody and study the relationship between the two. Quite often it will be found that the melody wishes to do one thing and the words another. The quality of this relationship often depends on whether the words or the melody were created first in the compositional process. Unless the wordsmith is accomplished at setting words to an already existing melody, it can be difficult to make a close connection between the pitches, durations and phrases implied by the melody and the natural rhythms, weighting and phrasing required by the words. This eternal pathway of two adjacent rivers of thought will be constantly changing its perspective and confluence in search of as perfect a match as possible.

If the melody at any point departs from the natural weighting of the words, It could naturally be assumed that either an error in composition has occurred, or the pitches or durations of the melody have been given priority for some good reason. One of course must be aware that it is not always the words that have been the inspiration for a composition. Sometimes lyricists are asked to set words to melodies and harmonies already created and have to make some compromises. Of course, some composers will also set words sometimes for a particular effect, or the words may be a translation. In conclusion, it is vital to be aware that weighting words as naturally as possible creates quality phrasing and increases the listeners' likelihood of understanding a message.

LEGATO

To continue this discussion concerning the importance of allowing the maximum meaning of a song to reveal itself, let us look at the concept of legato, which literally means smoothness. Although legato may often be viewed as the audible act of stringing together consecutive pitches as smoothly as possible, it is not done consciously but is more a consequence of insightful musical awareness and feeling. It is something that is allowed to reveal itself as an act of human and musical expression. What is often perceived by the listener as good legato in singing is really the result of effective weighting, breathing, pauses, word phrasing, and expressive dynamics, with a result that is misinterpreted by the listener as linear smoothness that travels through time. If of course there are no words present for the singer, then word weighting would not be contributing to the balance of the elements involved.

A desire to create a smooth vocal line through an over-preoccupation with the pitches of the melody can often be in natural opposition to the natural weighting of the words and can unintentionally create a more compromised and restricted vocal line which conflicts with the nature of the words.

So, to conclude, legato is much more an experience perceived by the listener, while from the singer's perspective it is the result of intelligent awareness and delivery of word weighting, breathing pauses, word phrases and the dynamic expression of the inner musical intelligence of the individual.

To try and achieve legato by artificially causing it to happen through control and conscious manipulation of sound durations and connections will often reveal itself as an inferior product. Quite often, what is perceived by the listener as good legato is in fact excellent mental continuity and intelligent understanding. Phrases may be audibly chopped up by unusual pauses and breaths and weighting of words, yet if there is an intelligent mental continuity present in the performer, then quite often the lyricism and connectivity of delivery may still express itself to the listener as a legato, or smooth passage of events.

ACCENT

Much of the time, singing in a regional or national accent does not adversely affect the meaning of the words or message in the song, if the performer gives due diligence to their study of song. Sometimes however, perhaps in folk, popular music or in musicals set in a specific national or local setting, compromises and considerations may need to be adopted in respect of the purpose of the respective piece. To this end it would be good practice to ensure that the flavour of the accent is clear enough to fulfil its purpose but also to give the words their due required clarity.

Examples would be the Cornish accent required in much of the singing in Gilbert & Sullivan's 'The Pirates of Penzance' or the hybrid London/Jewish accent required for the character of Fagin in 'Oliver' or even the awkward issue of singing a negro spiritual without giving the inappropriate pronunciations of the early black Americans, some of whom might typically have pronounced words such as 'the' as 'd' or 'dee'.

SINGING WITH OTHERS

When singing in unison or in harmony with others, it is vital to ensure that four key elements are in place. These are pitch, duration, articulation and vowel shape. Once the correct pitches have been produced by the group as a collective, the durations of pitches need to be checked also. After this, all members of the ensemble will need to articulate consonants and glottals at the same time and then ensure that the vowel shapes for words and the movement from vowel to vowel in all diphthongs is coordinated among the group. If getting this right is made a fundamental part of rehearsals, it is likely to greatly improve performance.

5

THE INVISIBLE CRAFT

There are experiences in life that we know, or feel, are true because we have experienced them. They are, however, difficult to explain to others without giving them the same experience. Elements of the invisible craft are as real as the visible and tangible but are experiences, perceptions or states of awareness rather than things that can be touched and measured with the tools of the physical world.

The elements of the invisible craft are not intellectual and cannot be forced to appear by sheer will. They are revealed to the seeking individual at the correct moment in time. These experiences are simple, yet profound in nature. They are logical, practical and powerful once known, and yet at times they are difficult to find. Patience and a relentless pursuit is required, with no force or demand. An open mind is also needed, and a trust that these perceptions are real and will eventually be revealed to the seeking individual.

THOUGHT

A thought, for example, is an invisible phenomenon which we also know as a very real thing. We do not know where thoughts come from, where they go to, why we sometimes cannot stop them and why we often cannot control them. Our response or reaction to them can often be measured scientifically by altered or elevated bodily functions, which often turn into what we would describe as feelings and emotions and may well manifest themselves physically as illness and ailments. But nevertheless, the thoughts themselves cannot be seen; they are invisible.

Brain activity may be observed with scientific equipment, but it cannot show the thoughts that create the activity in the first place. For reasons such as these, the individual must never underestimate the power of the intuitive yet invisible intelligence of the inner being and its ability to control the physical and expressive processes involved in the vocalising process. To allow the inner being to function as it wishes will be to allow most of the vocalising work for the individual to be carried out with comparative ease.

CONTROL THE SOURCE, NOT THE RESULT

The individual will often feel a very powerful, indeed virtually uncontrollable, desire to control the resulting sound he or she wishes for, but will only truly attain this aim by controlling the original perception of the creative process. This will always be something other than the result they wished for. A result can never be controlled; it can only be allowed to reveal itself by a focus on the events that create it.

CENTRED FOCUS

Of paramount importance for the singer is the requirement to seek and then allow an immovable focus on their own centre. It is achieved through an inward gaze, just as you might be still enough to mentally follow the beating of your own heart or the natural movement of your own breathing. With the breath, for example, the intention would be to watch the breath self-function, with no desire to influence or consciously cause the breath to occur at your own behest. The breath will be taken at a natural point, even though the individual might begin to show concern or even panic that the breathing process is not going to function as expected. If this 'watching' process were continued for a number of minutes, the individual would begin to feel a great sense of stillness and centredness with the mind's eye 'activated in stillness', so to speak, an apparent oxymoron and paradox and yet a very real event for the practitioner.

YOU AND IT

There is a point at the centre of the self which may be perceived by the mind's eye. When the focus of the mind reaches this point, the point disappears and becomes centred awareness. All the time the mind remains in this present moment, this is 'you'. From here *you* observe and monitor the workings of the subconscious, which manufactures the result initiated at the source by the conscious mind. This 'you' place is an aspect of the conscious mind, but does not require thought to exist; it is a state of awareness of the true self as opposed to the ego self, which is an artificial creation of the mind, a mental image we form of ourselves, of who we think we are based on personal and cultural conditioning. It consists of mind activity and can only perpetuate itself by constant thinking.

Now of course when we sing, we use thoughts, but we do not identify ourselves directly with the thinking aspect of mind. We utilise this thinking aspect from our still focus on the true self. Only when we sing from this state of awareness do our thoughts become truly creative. It is not the busy thinking mind which is creative but the still, true self 'non-thinking' aspect of mind.

Any distraction that causes the mind to consciously leave its centred point of focus 'you' is 'it'. The relationship between 'you' and 'it' must be maintained in order to allow the conscious self to stay focused in the present moment and the subconscious to take control of the result. Every time the focus moves to 'it', whatever that may be, the required focus on 'you' will be automatically lost. When this process is as it should be with the focus entirely on 'you', it feels like 'you' are watching yourself sing. The result you wish for is a consequence of the perceptions and intentions perceived at source.

PHYSICAL AND MENTAL SIGHT

To embed the inner focus 'you', the singer must differentiate between physical and mental sight. The physical eyes can look only at the world outside the individual, but the mind can perceive anything it wishes to, inside or outside the individual. As the singer begins to focus the attention of the mind's eye inwards, the difference between the physical and mental eyes becomes more apparent. As the mind looks in, the physical eyes try to look in but of course can only look out. This creates a battle of wills which the singer must pursue with unmovable intention until the physical and mental eyes work in partnership, each playing a different role from the other but an integral and synergistic one. In the end, the physical eyes 'see' out without 'looking', and the mind's eye 'sees' outside and inside the individual self as a consequence of 'looking' (directing its attention) inwards.

CONFIDENCE

Confidence is an invisible state of mind but it, or the lack of it, is deeply felt by the person experiencing it. It is a state of mind in which you expect a desired outcome to occur. You don't assume it will, and know that it may not, but nevertheless you assume it is likely based on tried and tested knowledge and previously practised outcomes; either that or you have a particularly optimistic outlook. If you lack confidence, by contrast, you focus on the likelihood of something you want to happen not happening. This is often experienced as a natural pessimism about the outcome. It is important therefore to try and test things until confidence reveals itself, and until that show of confidence occurs, it is often best to try and test things with an open heart and mind and accept all things along the way as stepping-stones to wisdom. It will be prudent for all individuals to beware, however, of having unjustified confidence, as this may well be unintentional self-delusion. I heard this beautifully phrased by the great actor and director Orson Welles when he described himself as a young man having the 'arrogance of ignorance'.

PROJECTION

Projection is another profoundly misunderstood concept. Generally when people speak of projection, they are referring to the ability of the performer to transfer in some way their voice, volume, words, intention or personality to an audience. It is sometimes referred to as 'stage presence'. It is not just about being loud enough; it has more to do with a person seeming closer than they are, or larger than life, or being perceived to be making a close connection with you, the observer.

For projection to be most powerfully effective, it is vital for the individual performer to do the opposite of what the audience may expect them to do. The fundamental misunderstanding about projection is that it is not something a performer does; it is something that happens as a direct consequence of the performer's perception. Although recognised and experienced, it cannot be seen or measured other than as an experience.

Projection is a state of awareness that is focused at the centre of the individual, but is mentally as big as the perceived arena. That is, the focus of personal attention and the size of the attention occupying the space outside the physical body are part of the same perception. If the performer wishes to fill a theatre, then their focus would be on the centre of themselves but the accompanying awareness is as big as the performance arena they perceive. In that way the performer is inviting the arena and the audience in, as opposed to reaching out *to* the audience. This manner of thinking opens the personality and allows full projection. The audience feels drawn to the performer; they feel closer and more connected. The individual performer cannot however cause this to happen by doing it consciously; it is a state of perception. Projection then is a state of awareness which is reflected outwards as a consequence of an inner focus which draws the listener inwards.

Projection occurs in much the same way as the phenomenon of daydreaming. When observing a person daydreaming, you can see that the perception in their eyes is expanded, as they are experiencing an intense and vivid preoccupation with the visions in their mind's eye. This of itself naturally draws you in as an observer. Most observers notice that it is much easier to be naturally drawn to look at a person in a crowd who is daydreaming than to those who are not. It is difficult to publicly daydream and not be noticed, for this very reason. The mind's eye is utterly aware of the space inside and outside the body, but it has a particular preoccupation with the visions of the mind. This is a perfect state for a singer to be in. It is exemplified by the description of the great actor Richard Burton, who was described as having "a cathedral in his eyes".

To allow projection to occur is to focus on every thought and perception being brought to the performing individual. Every member of the audience is mentally invited towards the performer. The aim is to never leave this centred point of focus. From here the audience is perceived to be in the palm of the performer's hand'. Projection is something to be explored as an individual; to place yourself in the daydreaming state and notice the effects, to walk into a room within the state of active and internal stillness and then observe how others respond to this state. There may well be a need to fight the desire to make it happen and remind oneself that it is not something that is done but is a consequence of a perception.

As the performer explores the relationship between the outward (physical) and inward (mental) eye, the tendency to find focus in a song may often lead to the singer closing the eyes. Remembering that the eyes are the 'mirrors of the soul', this is something to be concerned about. Although the closing of the eyes in performance may seem appropriate at times, it can easily become habitual and increase in frequency, or even become continuous, if not carefully monitored. It can quickly become a barrier between the performer and the audience, so it should not be overdone and should be monitored carefully when crafting and delivering a performance.

Some have been fortunate enough to experience those strange and wonderful moments in life when something they were doing seemed effortless and almost 'out of body', but for the singer this can become an everyday reality. Some singers wish to pursue the craft of singing to this deeper and life-altering level. In this state the inner being, in stillness and detachment, sees the singing result as a consequence of the intention to sing at source. The voice is revealed as a consequence of controlling the inner self and not the voice.

No human mind can consciously control the intricate complexity of physiology and psychology necessary to produce the singing phenomenon. This is because the egoic mind – which believes it can – will of its own desire only limit the capabilities of the individual to deliver what he or she wants to deliver. It does this by creating boundaries and belief systems which only inhibit and limit the true intelligence within, which is actually able to control the singing for us if given the freedom to do so. The singer will only truly control their own voice by giving up control of it and gaining a focus on the inner self.

6

PERFORMANCE

THE LANGUAGES OF MUSICAL INTERPRETATION

As the individual becomes more effective in their own singing, they will naturally begin to free creative insights that may have lain dormant, partially dormant or even blocked. As this freeing process evolves, they may naturally begin to establish a new or enhanced relationship with the music they are interacting with. This may entail an exploration of experiences and emotions from the past. It will certainly involve an exploration of words and word usage, the interplay between melody, harmony and rhythm and an involvement with the composer who created the music. The latter may be themselves or another, but the composer's intentions will certainly now influence their own.

Music's messages are normally found within the interplay of the elements we call pitch and duration. Separate pitches are called tunes, with the most important tunes being called melodies. In songs, singers predominantly sing the melody whilst supported by tunes layered into combinations of different simultaneous or overlapping pitches, which we call harmonies. Durations often contain regular pulses which are called the beat or pulse, whilst other durations are formed into different combinations of different length. which we call rhythms or patterns. These elements converse with each other and constantly alter their position of importance to illustrate different expressive qualities. For singers there is also the added element of words.

These elements express a vast array of emotions and it is important for the singer to become proficient in connecting harmonies with emotions and explore combining a performance of a melody with mentally feeling the underpinning emotions lying within the harmonies. So, for example, if a vocal melody is lacking in interest itself, then the underlying harmony may well be providing the emotional meaning.

ESTABLISH THE SONG'S PURPOSE

Every song has a purpose, and it is for the performer to discover what that purpose is and then look at every possible vehicle at their disposal to deliver that purpose. It may be to entertain, to move, to motivate, to celebrate, or to tell a story, which may do all these things. Discovering the purpose of the song should be your first port of call. The composer's or character's intention should be yours too.

Once the composer's intention and desire have been identified, you will know that the various aspects of the piece have been created to achieve that intention. By bringing the attention to that purpose, the performer will automatically be looking to reveal the most important features and in so doing will be realising the original motivation or vision. Every piece of music will have a function or purpose; to tell a story, to paint a picture, to make you dance, to make you happy or sad etc. Work out this purpose straight away and then look at the elements within the piece to assess the main vehicles for transportation of the purpose. It will normally be the tunes or melodies, the rhythmical features, the harmonies, the words or various combinations of the elements at given moments in time. Once discovered, it will then be the performer's purpose to try to reveal the qualities of musicality, intelligence and manner that will provide best support for the conveyance of that purpose.

Composers write songs because they feel compelled to; it is their nature and innate desire. Their reasons may be literary, musical, emotional or monetary, but whatever their reason, their need to create is from desire, whether selfish or unselfish.

The appeal of a song from a listener's viewpoint will be selective, based on the fact that they are individuals. As a singer I may well bias my listening towards the vocal aspect of a piece, whereas a guitarist would typically veer more towards the role of the guitar part. As individual listeners we decode performances according to our experiences and feelings about those experiences. When cutting through and beyond our natural leanings, when studying a piece as a performer, it is very important to take a broader look at the piece, as this often makes the difference between just churning out the expected rendition of a piece and the real artist who individualises a portrayal and studies to bring out the varied nuances hidden beneath the immediate surface.

ALLOW INTERPRETATION TO REVEAL ITSELF

It is vital to remember that to interpret in performance is not something that is done, but is a consequence of what is perceived. It is a mirror of what the performer understands and can allow themselves to reveal. For example, a performer cannot act love in a love song. They comprehend and perceive love within themselves, and as they hold on to that perception above their desire to convey it, the feeling will of itself be conveyed. As they *try* to convey it, they then lose it at source, and unintentionally act the emotion instead.

Although it is often the nature of an individual to want to convey the purpose of a song to an audience, it is essential to remember never to perform *out* to an audience – to attempt to 'sell' the song. The singer must always have an internal and immovable focus on the song and mentally invite the audience to them.

Although expression and emotion are of themselves invisible at source, they may be observed, sensed and felt by an audience. The performer perceives thoughts within himself or herself and then allows the ideas, emotions or experiences to manifest themselves to the external world. The audience, as fellow humans, then recognise the same experience within themselves, and a shared connection is made. Body language manifests in the same way and may be conscious and unconscious.

Although performing to others is a craft in itself, many people are frightened at the thought of performing in front of an audience. The good news is that they don't have to. It does provide an added dimension, but it is not essential; sometimes singing is a personal experience, and that is fine also.

Once a decision has been made to perform a song however, there must be a constant scrutiny as to what the singer *is* and *is not* allowing to happen. It is so easy for the performer to try too hard and get in their own way. The challenge is to create a healthy balance of being watchful, vigilant, perceptive, pernickety and patient but *not* demanding or judgemental. The latter can often cause anxiety and thoughts of hopelessness and frustration, and may well manifest the very blocks the individual is trying to avoid. The process should be very 'simple', which again should not be confused with 'easy'.

WHAT SHOULD I SING?

We all have a distinctive quality of sound which makes it difficult for our voice to suit every style of music. We may be able to perform in a particular style very well without it really suiting us, but at some point we need to accept the fact that we will be most effective if we match our natural sound qualities with our personality and musical preferences and then match these with the type of singing that most suits us. This is merely a process of recognising and flowing with acoustic law and fusing this with our natural sound and style preferences.

Too many people have harmed their voices unnecessarily in their pursuit of styles of vocalising unsuited to their natural makeup, and however unpalatable this may be, this should be a vital consideration for any singer wishing for success and longevity in the field. Once the performer has also assessed the main qualities of voice with regard to range, weight, colour and size, then they will be much more likely to maximise their likelihood of success and fulfilment.

TESSITURA

The 'tessitura' of a piece of music may be a very important point to consider when selecting a song. The tessitura refers to the general lie of the notes to be sung with regard to pitch and not necessarily just the range or compass of notes. A song may contain notes mostly in the singer's middle range but include a few high sustained notes, but the tessitura of the piece over all would be comfortable. On the other hand, a piece may contain a fairly small range of notes, which tend to lie consistently high in pitch. For this reason, it may be a more difficult piece to sing unless the top range is a particularly strong feature of the voice.

TRANSFER THE PRINCIPLES BETWEEN SONGS

Effective singing, like effective living, is underpinned by principles, i.e. building blocks that work together to create a product. The beautiful thing about focusing on principles is that even though the singer may be studying to sing one particular phrase, the principles underneath the music to varying degrees are part of *all* the songs they will ever sing. The principles will just be adjusting their importance at any given time. For this reason, the singer must make sure that as they move from phrase to phrase or piece to piece, they take the principles with them. They may be applying them to different situations, but the underlying principles will still be present. Ensuring transference of the principles is what matters.

SINGING WITH INSTRUMENTS

If the singer is playing an instrument at the same time as singing, then it becomes very important to establish the correct balance of the two instruments based on the role the singing plays in the respective composition. If the performer is a backing singer and the vocals are an additional part to an instrumental piece, then it would seem appropriate to allow the voice to play a supporting role. If the piece is a song, however, the requirement would be for the singing to take dominance and priority. The singers will need to understand the purpose of the piece first and then decide on the best vehicles for transportation of that purpose. A guitarist, for example, who begins to write and perform their own songs will probably need to decide whether they are wishing to be a guitarist with added vocals or a singer with guitar accompaniment. If it is primarily a song, then really the narrative and vocal part has to take priority unless there is good reason for it not to.

PRACTICE

It is always best to practice anything regularly. Better to practice for five or 10 minutes every day rather than half an hour twice a week. It is also vital to ensure as much as possible that the focus is on the quality of the practice. Ten minutes of good quality practice is preferable to 20 minutes of mixed quality practice. A good general principle also would be to continually find things to practise of good quality which will naturally help the singer to replace the poor habits that may have already shown themselves. To try *not* to do something already places the mind in a negative frame of mind. It should be like overwriting poor software with a superior version.

Even better than planning regular practice slots in a given day would be to practise certain elements throughout the day. As it has already been stated that speaking and singing should be viewed in the same way, in many respects it would behove the singing practitioner to speak throughout the day, employing many of the singing principles in their everyday speech. This would certainly help merge the two concepts together in a very natural way.

7

TEACHING

THE NATURAL SINGER AND TEACHING

In the end, most singers who do well are in many ways natural. They have little knowledge of how they do what they do. They will often do well regardless of the teacher they have, even though the teacher may try to take responsibility for what their student produces.

It is also very difficult for the natural singer to explain to others what they themselves do. This typically makes them poor teachers. Because they can do it, that does not necessarily mean that they can teach it. When asked, a natural singer may describe to another what they feel they themselves are doing to improve an aspect of their own singing. Because the natural singer is making modifications and finding success in accordance with their own makeup however, this does not necessarily mean that the same application of a technique will automatically work for another singer.

WHAT TO LOOK FOR IN A TEACHER

What is important for a teacher is what they know, and *where* they can bring a student *from* and take them *to.* It also takes less effort from a teacher to take an already naturally gifted singer and performer on to success than for them to take somebody with minimal talent and understanding on to even moderate success.

When looking for a teacher, my advice is to listen to and observe everyone and everything, but be aware of short-term fixes. There may be many approaches that have short-term success built in. Short term however is not long term, and such remedies may well lead to time and money unwisely spent. Finding a hundred ways *not* to do something will be that much closer to finding what is right. In fact, some of the most frustrating and seemingly unproductive lessons can long term prove to be the most insightful lessons, and quite often, the results of any graft may well appear unexpectedly at a later date.

A good singing teacher should be able to teach every voice, style and age. This is because under all good singing there are fundamental principles that should accommodate all circumstances.

The quality of a teacher cannot be measured by a grade or a mark out of ten, or even by word of mouth. The teacher must be appraised by the individual student. Because singers are individuals with different requirements for self-development, it may be useful to try a number of teachers short term and perhaps a few or one or two long term. If a fantastic teacher can be found then great, but there may also be a need for some coaching or support in a particular field short term; perhaps an accompanist, some help with 'note bashing' or help with languages, a particular style or microphone technique.

Over time, you will pick up many other techniques of performance through observation of others and personal practice. They will typically include accommodating your style of address to the occasion, the venue and the type of audience, striking that balance between formal and friendly, knowing how and when to move around the stage and when to stay still. In classical music the singer's stance is nearly always standing, but it can vary; sometimes you may adopt a symmetrical stance with the weight distributed equally between your feet, while for more informal songs the weight can be biased to one side and the weight shifted to the other side to fit in with the various shifts in the narrative of the story being told. In popular music the singer may be standing or sitting on a stool, and they may be playing guitar or piano. When performing with others the singer will need to work out when to look at their fellow performers and when to look to the audience. Body angles will need to be planned, and you'll need to stand in the correct place for the lighting.

When seeking a teacher, the individual student must certainly not be unduly swayed by how well known or famous the teacher is or what students they produce. There are many ways to become a successful teacher; by luck, timing, fate, merit, who you are, who you know or by selecting the best students in the first place.

The art of teaching is to reveal the true and honest nature of a person. This will include their sound, feelings, thoughts and personality. Only then will the singer have true integrity. A singer will of course be influenced and inspired by others but should always aim to sound unique – after all, they *are*.

BEWARE THE TEACHER

Beware the teacher who churns out students who sound the same or similar; there is bound to be something contrived or unnatural in the teaching process they use.

Beware the teacher who is a pianist or instrumentalist who has picked up all sorts of 'bits and bobs' over the years and professes that this makes them a singing teacher.

There is a difference between a 'teacher' and a 'coach'. Coaches can guide and advise on performing, repertoire, tips, style etc but to know how to sing properly you will need a teacher.

In many respects the terms' teacher' and 'coach' are a matter of semantics. From my perspective as a singing teacher, I will help a student to become a better singer or vocalist by giving them information and experiences that they will then apply to become better singers. I see a coach as someone who may have the knowledge needed to help someone improve, but when coaching they will be focussing on guiding an individual in a specific area of the craft, such as microphone technique or singing in a foreign language. This means that some individuals are teachers who can also coach in a specialist area, while other coaches may only be able to advise on specific specialist areas without being able to teach the comprehensive craft of a singing teacher.

Beware the teacher who can only teach classical singing or only popular singing, or only men, or only women, or only children, or only adults. There are fundamental principles to all singing and a teacher of worth will have a flexible approach to accommodate all styles, all ages and all voice types. However that does not mean to say that a teacher who tends to specialise in one of these groups *can* only teach these people well; they may have chosen to focus on one 'market sector' because they are best known for it, or because it's a convenient use of their contacts.

POSTSCRIPT

Singing is a fundamentally natural process. Quality singing is not just voice but an integral part of the most amazing creative process. The singer's only concern must be with the source of this process, so that the resulting sound may reveal itself in its purest form.

The singing *result* must never be directly controlled, and all thoughts of so doing must be relinquished. It is only in relinquishing control of the result that the singer truly *gains* control of it. In freeing the voice in this way, the singer frees themselves.

At the heart of this sea of creative thinking is a great stillness. This is *you*, and within this stillness the inner being reveals itself. Then *you* will view singing from within and observe yourself singing as if it were a separate but connected aspect of a whole.

There are many mental pathways to this stillness which need to be travelled regularly. As these pathways approach the stillness they dissolve and become absorbed into a single state of awareness but reappear as the individual loses their way and re-travels the routes again.

The journey is difficult, although fundamentally simple, but it will reveal more about the individual and the singing process than you might imagine.

It is not the aim of this book to prove that all this information is true. In fact, can any of us prove anything is true? In the end we all have access to facts and experiences; we then decide for ourselves what we consider to be the truth. The truth as we perceive it will also change for us as we journey through life. The aim therefore is to provide the reader with information that will lead to experiences, so that they may discover for themselves what they consider to be the truth.

ABOUT THE AUTHOR

Ashley Kirkham GRNCM LRAM ARCM LGSM PGCE is a professional singer, singing teacher and school music teacher. He studied at the Royal Northern College of Music in Manchester where he gained his graduate Diploma in performance. He was a member of the William Byrd singers, the BBC Northern Singers, sang roles in College Operas and country wide solo concert work as well as gaining three further Performance Diplomas from the Guildhall, Royal academy and Royal Colleges of music in London.

After leaving college he chose to pursue a career combining work as a specialist one-to-one singing teacher, Head of music in High school and middle school, specialist work with private clients and specialist music schools, his own professional performances and writing about the craft of singing. This book is the culmination of fifty years of study.

BV - #0107 - 060622 - C0 - 203/127/7 - PB - 9781861519481 - Gloss Lamination